Mel Bay Presents Stefan Grossman's Guitar Workshop Audio Series

Folk and Blues
Fingerstyle Guitar
taught by Dave Van Ronk

CONTENTS

The Compact Disc lessons accompanying this book are taken from the video lessons of the same title.

Visit us on the Web at www.melbay.com — E-mail us at email@melbay.com

CD Track Listings
Lesson One

Track 1: Intro to *Green, Green, Rocky Road*
Track 2: Performance of *Green, Green, Rocky Road*
Track 3: Talk about *Green, Green, Rocky Road*
Track 4: Tuning
Track 5: Teaching first section of *Green, Green, Rocky Road*
Track 6: Plays first section of *Green, Green, Rocky Road*
Track 7: Teaching second section of *Green, Green, Rocky Road*
Track 8: Plays second section of *Green, Green, Rocky Road*
Track 9: Teaches chorus of *Green, Green, Rocky Road*
Track 10: Plays *Green, Green, Rocky Road* slowly
Track 11: Plays *Green, Green, Rocky Road* up to tempo
Track 12: Teaching of ending for *Green, Green, Rocky Road*
Track 13: Talk on guitar as accompaniment instrument
    and playing in different keys
Track 14: Teaching phrases for *Kansas City Blues*

Track 15: Performance of *Kansas City Blues*
Track 16: Performance of *Saturday Night Shuffle*
Track 17: Teaching first section of *Saturday Night Shuffle*
Track 18: Plays slowly first section of *Saturday Night Shuffle*
Track 19: Discusses accenting on first section of *Saturday Night Shuffle*
Track 20: Teaching second section of *Saturday Night Shuffle*
Track 21: Plays beginning of second section of *Saturday Night Shuffle*
Track 22: Continues teaching of second section of *Saturday Night Shuffle*
Track 23: Plays from F chord of *Saturday Night Shuffle*
Track 24: Plays *Saturday Night Shuffle* at tempo
Track 25: Intro to *Stackerlee*
Track 26: Performance of *Stackerlee*
Track 27: Teaching of *Stackerlee*
Track 28: Plays *Stackerlee*
Track 29: Closing thoughts

Lesson Two

Track 1: Intro to *Ballad of the IRT*
Track 2: Performance of *Ballad of the IRT*
Track 3: Tuning
Track 4: Teaching first section of *Ballad of the IRT*
Track 5: Teaching second section of *Ballad of the IRT*
Track 6: Plays slowly *Ballad of the IRT*
Track 7: Plays *Ballad of the IRT* up to tempo
Track 8: Intro to *Wilson Rag*
Track 9: Performance of *Wilson Rag*
Track 10: Teaching of *Wilson Rag*
Track 11: Plays slowly *Wilson Rag*
Track 12: Continues teaching of *Wilson Rag*
Track 13: Plays *Wilson Rag* up to tempo
Track 14: Intro to *That Will Never Happen No More*

Track 15: Performance of *That Will Never Happen No More*
Track 16: Teaching of verse to *That Will Never Happen No More*
Track 17: Teaching of chorus to *That Will Never Happen No More*
Track 18: Plays slowly G to E7 phrase
Track 19: Continues teaching of chorus to *That Will Never Happen No More*
Track 20: Teaching of descending bass line
Track 21: Plays slowly *That Will Never Happen No More*
Track 22: Plays *That Will Never Happen No More* up to tempo
Track 23: Intro to *Spike Driver's Moan*
Track 24: Performance of *Spike Driver's Moan*
Track 25: Teaching of *Spike Driver's Moan*
Track 26: Plays *Spike Driver's Moan* up to tempo
Track 27: Closing thoughts

Lesson Three

Track 1: Intro to *Sportin' Life Blues*
Track 2: Performance of *Sportin' Life Blues*
Track 3: Tuning
Track 4: Teaching of beginning of guitar accompaniment
    to verse to *Sportin' Life Blues*
Track 5: Plays guitar accompaniment to verse to *Sportin' Life Blues*
Track 6: Continues teaching guitar accompaniment to verse
    to *Sportin' Life Blues*
Track 7: Plays guitar accompaniment to verse to *Sportin' Life Blues*
    from top to turnaround
Track 8: Teaching of turnaround to *Sportin' Life Blues*
Track 9: Plays guitar accompaniment to verse to *Sportin' Life Blues*
Track 10: Plays first guitar break to *Sportin' Life Blues*
Track 11: Teaching of first phrase to first guitar break to *Sportin' Life Blues*
Track 12: Plays first phrase to first guitar break to *Sportin' Life Blues*
Track 13: Teaching of G phrase to first guitar break to *Sportin' Life Blues*
Track 14: Plays G phrase to first guitar break to *Sportin' Life Blues*
Track 15: Teaching from Gm chord to end of first guitar break
    to *Sportin' Life Blues*
Track 16: Plays guitar accompaniment to verse and first guitar break
Track 17: Plays second guitar break to *Sportin' Life Blues*

Track 18: Teaching of first four bars to second guitar break
    to *Sportin' Life Blues*
Track 19: Plays first four bars to second guitar break to *Sportin' Life Blues*
Track 20: Continues teaching from end of fourth bar to second guitar break
    to *Sportin' Life Blues*
Track 21: Plays all parts of arrangement to *Sportin' Life Blues*
Track 22: Intro to *St. James Infirmary*
Track 23: Performance of *St. James Infirmary*
Track 24: Teaching of accompaniment to vocal to *St. James Infirmary*
Track 25: Plays accompaniment to vocal to *St. James Infirmary*
Track 26: Teaching of first instrumental break to *St. James Infirmary*
Track 27: Plays first instrumental break to *St. James Infirmary*
Track 28: Plays second instrumental break to *St. James Infirmary*
Track 29: Teaching of first phrase of second instrumental break
    to *St. James Infirmary*
Track 30: Plays first phrase of second instrumental break
    to *St. James Infirmary*
Track 31: Continues teaching of second instrumental break
    to *St. James Infirmary*
Track 32: Teaching of end phrase of second instrumental break
    to *St. James Infirmary*

A conversation with Dave Van Ronk
By David Walsh

Photo by Jo Ayres

Few folk or blues enthusiasts of my generation need to be introduced to Dave Van Ronk, the extraordinary singer and guitarist. His name is inextricably linked, first and foremost, to the folk music scene in New York City's Greenwich Village in the 1960s. He played with and knew virtually everyone of musical significance in that decade.

Van Ronk, born in Brooklyn on June 30, 1936, has been performing for more than four decades. He made his first record for Moses Asch's Folkways label in 1959 and gained widespread recognition for his recordings with Prestige in the 1960s. He performed at countless festivals, such as the annual Newport event, and toured the US and internationally. A compilation of those early recordings, The Folkways Years, 1959-1961, is available from Smithsonian/Folkways. His most recent recording, From ... Another Time and Place (1995) was released on Alcazar Records.

Van Ronk continues to perform, as well as teach guitar. I saw him at a club in Ann Arbor in late 1997. He plays the sort of music he likes, with small regard for the boundaries that normally separate jazz and blues and country and folk. He proves in practice that those distinctions don't mean very much. His performances now are stripped down to the essentials: emotional and musical honesty. He is a unique individual and musical figure. I spoke to him recently in Greenwich Village, where he still lives.

DW: What were the social circumstances under which you grew up?

DVR: If you asked anybody in my family, they would have very stridently proclaimed themselves middle class. My mother and father were separated, so he doesn't count. My mother was a stenographer, a stenographer-typist. My uncle and my grandfather both worked in the Brooklyn Navy Yard. He was an electrician and subsequently became something of an aristocrat of labor. My great grandfather admired Eugene V. Debs. My great grandmother hated Debs because she said he was leading my great grandfather off the straight and narrow, and getting him drunk. She was probably right. In any event, the family, mostly Irish, was working class. I was born in Bushwick, but I grew up in Richmond Hill, in Queens. I went to Catholic school.

DW: What was that like?

DVR: Horrible. The nuns were ignorant, if not mean. There was Sister Attila Maria, for example. These were vicious Irish nuns.

Oh, I got along with some of them.

DW: What did you read as a kid?

DVR: It depends what age. I remember reading Grant's memoirs, the autobiography of Buffalo Bill. Lots of Mark Twain. A massive book called Land and Sea, some sort of anthropological study. I read Hemingway at 13, The Sun Also Rises, which bored me. My brain was like the attic of the Smithsonian. They left me pretty much on my own. I began hanging out in pool halls.

When I was 15 or so, a truant officer picked me up in a pool hall. Actually, he was there for the guy I was playing with. I was hauled before the principal. You never saw the principal, this was like being brought before Stalin. He called me "a filthy ineducable little beast." That's a direct quote. You don't forget something like that. They basically said that if I didn't show up for school they'd mark me present, they wouldn't send the truant officer after me. At 16 I enrolled in something called continuing education. Once a month I'd go out to Jamaica, but I didn't take it seriously.

By this time I was listening to music, to jazz. Bebop, modern jazz mostly. But I leaned to the traditional jazz. That had its pluses and minuses. I cut myself off from the mainstream of jazz. It stood me in good stead later on, as a musician.

I started sitting in, playing the guitar, at clubs, like the Stuyvesant Casino, Childs' Paramount. Coleman Hawkins would come in, Johnny Hodges. There is an apprenticeship system in jazz. You teach the young ones. So even if the musicians weren't personally that likable, they felt an obligation to help the younger musicians. I played on the bandstand. I wasn't a member of the AF of M [musicians' union], of course. There would be somebody, like Jimmy Rushing, who would start singing if the union delegate came in, and you'd take off. Of course, your instrument was still up there. The delegate knew, but he wouldn't do anything about it.

DW: How did your recording career begin?

DVR: I was playing at a club. Odetta was performing there and she heard me. She said I was good. "Do you do this full-time?" "No, I'm a seaman." And I liked shipping out. "Well, you should," she said. "Why don't you make a demo tape? I'll send it to Albert Grossman." He owned a club in Chicago, and later managed Bob Dylan. Well, it wasn't so easy to make a demo tape in those days. But somehow I managed it. And I sent it to her. I hunkered down to wait. And I waited. Nothing happened. Finally, I hitchhiked to Chicago, in 24 hours, staying awake with Benzedrine. I was in bad shape when I got there. I got to Grossman's club, and, as luck would have it, he was there. He had never received any tape. But since I was there, he said, "Why don't you do an audition?" So I did. And when I was finished, I said, "Well?" He said, "I book Big Bill Broonzy in here, and Sonny Terry and Brownie McGhee. Why should I hire you?" And I blew up, I shouted, "You SOB, Grossman, you're Crowjimming me [practicing reverse racism]." And I went back to New York. But on the way, I got pickpocketed. I was sleeping, and one of my rides picked my pocket and stole my seaman's papers. That's why I'm a folk singer.

DW: Tell me a little bit more about the "golden era," as you described it. How did you experience the boom in the early sixties?

DVR: It was pretty weird. All of a sudden there was money all over the place. If there was ever any truth to the trickle-down theory, the only evidence of it I've ever seen was in that period of 1960 to 1965. All of sudden they were handing out major label recording contracts like they were coming in Cracker Jack boxes. People who had been sleeping on floors and eating in cafeterias a year or two before, all of a sudden had enough money to buy a suit, if they wanted to. And musically it was very interesting. It attracted a large number of talented people, who probably wouldn't have been interested in folk music had it not been so popular. Someone like Jose Feliciano. He played the guitar, he sang, ergo, he was a folk singer. Folk City, Gaslight, the Newport Folk Festival. There was a tremendous attraction for that brief period. Bob Dylan was another.

DW: When did you first meet him?

DVR: The winter of 1961-62, when he first came to New York.

DW: What was he like at that time?

DVR: Nervous. Nervous energy, he couldn't sit still. And very, very evasive. You never could pin him down on anything; he had a lot of stories about who he was and where he came from. He never seemed to be able to get them straight. What impressed me the most about him was his genuine love for Woody Guthrie. In retrospect, even he says now that he came to New York to "make it." That's BS. When he came to New York there was no folk music, no career possible, it was out of the question, it simply wasn't going to happen. What he said at the time is the story I believe. He came because he had to meet Woody Guthrie. And he used to go out to the hospital where Woody, who had Huntington's Chorea, stayed. He was slowly but surely sinking. And Bobby used to go out there two or three times a week and sit there, and play songs for him. In that regard he was as stand-up a cat as anyone I've ever met. That's also what got him into writing songs. He wrote songs for Woody, to amuse him, to entertain him. He also wanted Woody's approval.

DW: Could he communicate that approval?

DVR: His communication by the time Bobby showed up was at a minimum. But he could make himself understood if you were very patient. I believe Bobby did establish enough of a rapport to be able to do that.

DW: Did you like his music?

DVR: Yes, very much. It had what I call a gung-ho, unrelenting quality, a take-no-prisoners approach that was really very effective. He acquired very, very devoted fans among the other musicians before he had written his first song.

4

DW: Who were some of the other people who impressed you at the time?

DVR: There were a lot of them. Janis Ian. She was such a good musician. For one thing, the level of musicianship in the folk community was pretty low. So you could be Johann Sebastian Bach and it wouldn't be noticed. Curiously enough, it had its up side too. Nobody got zapped for being too sophisticated. Janis had a sophisticated melodic, chord sense. I knew her when she made Society's Child, before it became a hit. It just so happened that we were recording for the same label. She was 17 at the time.

Ian and Sylvia, who, when you got right down to it, were essentially country and western singers. I just recorded his Four Strong Winds. It's a wonderful song. It was the first thing he ever wrote. If my first song had been like that, I probably would have been afraid to write a second one. I used to be a pin setter when I was a kid, in a bowling alley, before they had the machines. On slow nights I used to bowl. I was terrible, the worst. But one night, I don't know what got into me, I bowled a turkey, three consecutive strikes. I have not picked up a bowling ball since.

DW: You mentioned in passing the civil rights movement. Did you ever go to the South?

DVR: No, I didn't. I worked with Jim Farmer and CORE here. I did this, that and the other thing. Mostly I did benefits, which is essentially what I do best. But when they needed a warm body, I presented them with mine for whatever it was worth.

DW: When you speak about the money, or the recording contracts, that became available, did you ever feel there was a moment when you had to make certain choices?

DVR: If you generate $100,000, is there anything wrong with asking for $35,000?

DW: I shouldn't have put it that way. Did you ever feel that you could put yourself in a situation where you would change?

DVR: No. The thought never entered my head. And for good reason. I've been very, very prosperous and I've been very, very poor, all in the last 20 or 30 years, and I don't see that my weltanschauung has been very much influenced. I'm a very, very stubborn man. You can't be afraid of failure and you can't be afraid of success, because either one gets in the way of your work. I formed a rock and roll band in 1965. Frankly, I was making a grab for the brass ring. I couldn't see any reason why not. Subsequently, I saw reasons why not. I found it musically boring and I quit, even though it was my band. Maybe we didn't give it enough of a chance, or something along that line. Maybe we needed better representation, or this, that and the other thing. But that isn't why I left. I left because I got tired of doing the same goddamn songs every night.

DW: What were some of the best experiences, the most satisfying experiences performing?

DVR: Some of them were in very small places. The first time I ever worked the Club 47 in Cambridge, Mass. No, I didn't actually work there the particular time I'm thinking of. I was up there just visiting Jim Kweskin, of the jug band. The next thing I know I'm bombed out of my mind on the stage at the Club 47 where I could never get arrested before. And I'm up there, I don't know what I'm doing, I'm just watching my fingers. Wow, they move and everything. I get off the stage and the manager comes over, "I didn't know how good you were, you want a job?" I found the missing ingredient to get hired at the Club 47 apparently. It's the incongruous things that stick in your head, not the great, wonderful ... the standing ovation you got in Nova Scotia in 1972, the great review you got in the Times. It's the quirky things that I remember, like down in Philadelphia I had to do some kind of early morning TV show. For some reason it was called Aqua something or other.

DW: It wasn't done under water.

DVR: It would have been better. So they sent a car for me to take me to the show, it's an aquarium. And it's one of these teenage dance shows. They have these huge fish tanks all around. They didn't have the facilities to do live broadcasting. So you had to lip synch. I had never done that before. Furthermore, even if I had done it before, it wouldn't have helped. I don't phrase my songs the same way twice; I try not to anyway. All I remember really is kids dancing, and as they go by the camera flipping the camera the finger. I remember saying, "Actually, I only came here to see the piranha, but you'll do." Those are the things.

DW: Did they dance to your music?

DVR: Yeah. They would have danced to an amplified cricket. They were there to boogie.

DW: This is in the 60s.

DVR: Yeah, it was one of those Dick Clark-type shows. At the time, I was outraged. I tried not to let it show. The first time I told the story and everybody started to laugh, I realized it was a wonderful thing. Only in America.

DW: What about the Newport Folk Festival, what was that like?

DVR: I never liked those things. I never liked the musical aspect of it. There was no focus, for one thing, too many things were going on at once. It was a three-ring circus. During the afternoon there'd be three or four concerts going on, and the sound overlapping. You couldn't even really hear what you came to hear. Put yourself in my position, or any singer's position, how would you like to sing for 15,000 people with frisbees? No focus. It was better at night, on the main stage at night, because there is a bit more focus, there was only one thing going on. The audience does tend to concentrate on what's happening on stage. So that was a little bit better. There were performers who thrived on that kind of thing. I never did. Pete Seeger, with every thousand people they added, he'd get better.

DW: What do you think of him and his music?

DVR: Oh, he's a wonderful musician. He's another guy who has been shortchanged as a musician. He's a very good musician and a very good singer. He phrases well. What am I supposed to say about the guy who invented my profession? And he did. He and Burl Ives, I suppose. I don't do the kind of music Pete does, but if you listen to that first solo album, that's a musical milestone. That stands to this day.

DW: What did you think of Joni Mitchell?

DVR: I thought she was about the best songwriter of the 60s. A remarkable sensibility, a good lyricist. Sometimes she lets the tricks get out of hand. She plays too obviously with things like alliteration and internal rhyming. It's that kind of playfulness, even in her serious songs, that give her material its je ne sais quoi. She is a very playful lyricist. I like that. John Donne was a very playful lyricist.

DW: After 1965 or so, did things decline?

DVR: Well, you know they kept on going in the form of folk-rock, but as far as the folk revival was concerned, it was pretty much over. I played in the same places. The business kept prospering right until 1969 or 1970. Until the whole hippie thing became manifestly the nightmare that it had always been. And then business got very bad. In the early 1970s. 1971, '72. The rooms were closing down, record labels weren't signing acoustic acts any more. Although they had been pretty much been getting out of that for some time before that. The shock of Richard Nixon. That guy was pretty demoralizing. The whole raison d'être of the New Left had been exposed as a lot of hot air, that was demoralizing. I mean, these kids thought they were going to change the world, they really did. They were profoundly deluded. I used to talk to them, to the hippies, yippies. I under-stood their mentality as well as anyone could. But things like Altamont, things like Kent State, the election of Richard Nixon, the fact that the war just kept going on and on and on, and nothing they did could stop it. Phil Ochs wrote the song, I declare the war is over, that was despair, sheer despair. By the mid-70s, I wanted to get out of the business. I was tired anyway.

DW: Had you continued recording?

DVR: Oh, yeah. I don't think I went a year or so without a record between 1959 and 1979, sometimes two. I got in under the wire, so I could keep on trundling along, although on a much lower level in terms of income. But by 1976 I hung it up for a while. To hell with this. I hung out my shingle. I taught guitar for a year or so. Performing is addictive. After a year or so, I was so antsy, in spite of the fact that I hadn't changed my mind about the pluses or minuses of doing it.

DW: What is it you enjoy most about performing?

DVR: Well, you know, it's very hard to put it into words. If I could put it into words, I'd be a writer. If I do a piece in my living room, if I practice it—and I have the tapes to prove this—it's not going to be as good as doing the same piece in front of an audience. When you're working in front of an audience, you have incentive to excel. When you're working for yourself, you don't have that incentive. Part of it is fear, which supplies a good deal of adrenaline. Part of it is sheer hamminess. I'm an exhibitionist, I was an exhibitionist as a kid.

One of my earliest memories ... I knew three full verses of the Star Spangled Banner when I was seven or eight years old. And one of the nuns discovered this phenomenon and I was actually sent around from classroom to classroom to do the whole thing. Let me tell you, I was not the most popular kid in school after that happened. Like the kid who memorized the most scripture in Tom Sawyer. I was a ham. Now, you know, I'm not so much. You get it out of your system. Whatever it is you have to prove, you prove.

I was talking to a friend of mine, a psychoanalyst. For some reason, we were talking about Jack the Ripper. His theory was that the reason why Jack the Ripper disappeared, was never caught, was because he cured himself. He'd gone through it, and after a few murders, he was no longer crazy. The performer is much like Jack the Ripper. After a while you get it out of your system and you're not nearly the exhibitionist that you were when you started out. By that time you've acquired the skills. I still enjoy it.

DW: Do you think that art or music is a way of knowing the world, of experiencing the world?

DVR: I don't think you're dealing with the same thing in the arts that you're dealing with in life. Except insofar as it is a way of organizing things. It is no more like life than chess is like life. And yet some of the skills that you acquire, a way of thinking, a way of addressing problems, will carry over into the way you organize your life, the way you look at the world. Most of it's done on a subconscious level. If you look at music, you see theme, variation, you see symmetry, asymmetry, you see structure, and these are related to skills in the real world. I think I have more in common with a carpenter than you might think. We're putting things together. That aspect of it does relate to the real world in a parallel way. In the sense that two parallel lines never meet, but they are nonetheless parallel. Which is why some of the greatest musicians are the greatest screw-ups.

DW: What sort of music still interests you the most?

DVR: Jazz. Most of what I listen to now is mainstream jazz from 1935 right up to and including early bebop and cool jazz. I get off at hard bop. Didn't like it at the time, still don't like it. Modern jazz per se is fine. I'm not put off by the weird changes, they're not weird, not to me. Modern Jazz Quartet, Gillespie, Parker, a lot of Teddy Wilson. A lot of the vocalists, Billie Holliday and some others who got lost in the shuffle.

DW: Do you think that it is inevitable that there is such a wall between so-called popular music and so-called classical music?

DVR: That's a very, very complicated question. What you're asking is a historical question, a question of the sociology of music. In this country that is an incredibly complex thing. We are a nation of immigrants. People came here with a body of music that

Dave Van Ronk & Stefan Grossman

Photo by Jo Ayres

was not viable. They were in the market, so to speak, for music that was viable. Very early on, consumer capitalism came to their rescue, with the very thing. That started to happen right after the Civil War and became the mainstream of American music before the turn of the century. So that classical, serious orchestral music, whatever you want to call it, never really had a shot.

Also, you have to bear in mind that classical music has been music of the ruling class since its inception. Monteverdi wasn't writing for the people. If he had, he would have starved to death. It's an elite musical form, which casts no inherent aspersions on it. This is a socio-musicological fact. Its history militates against it here. This is a very egalitarian country, and the very idea of there being such a thing as an elite with its own music is anathema to most Americans. How would one go about bridging that? Certain feckless attempts were made in the 1930s and 40s by CBS, NBC and so on. I remember listening to opera live on the radio from the Met [Metropolitan Opera]. I think it was on Saturday afternoons, with Milton Cross. I liked it, but I was a weird kid and I liked weird stuff. But early on I heard Oscar Levant's definition of opera, which you may or may not have heard: It's a play where everybody gets stabbed, but instead of bleeding, they sing. I think most Americans, if you wrote that out, they'd sign it. Would it be possible, if somehow or other, consumer capitalism...?

DW: Let's say, in a better society.

DVR: It's really hard to say. One of the problems would be the problem of continuity. A revolutionary period is not a good period for the arts. Now what we've got going right now is hardly a good period for the arts. You tack a revolutionary period on to what we've got now, and you're going to see a cultural breakdown of the very first order, I suspect, and whatever emerges is going to have to emerge ... you're going to have to quite literally bring to birth a new world from the ashes of the old. What grows from there, it's very hard to say, with that continuity shattered something new might arise, totally different from anything you could imagine. When you look at the mathematical possibilities of music, you realize that the way the West has taken it is far from the only way to go. I've always like Trotsky's writings as an art critic, possibly the only Trotskyist who really did understand the essentials of the field.

DW: The attempt is to initiate a discussion on social and artistic perspectives... you can't, you don't want to, tell people what to do. You can, I think, direct people's attention toward what you think is more interesting material. In any case, how does consciousness affect an artist? Does it help to have a correct political perspective? It does in general, but it doesn't necessarily make you a better painter. I would like to think that ultimately it would influence your work in some way or other.

DVR: I'm not sure it does. In my field the only way that politics can influence you is if you start singing political songs.

DW: Even directing people toward honesty or authenticity.

DVR: What you need is a whole, well-rounded historical approach to art.

DW: I agree.

DVR: You have to start with the Babylonians, the Egyptians, and right on through to the Romantics and the modernists. It's as much a life's work as politics.

DW: Absolutely.

DVR: The problem arises of priorities. With the system going haywire, running amok like it's doing now, can a political organization spare the personnel, the time, the energy? It's not a decision for me to make, thank god.

DW: We think so. We view the cultural questions as profoundly bound up with the social questions. The Russian Revolution wasn't simply the product of a political program, but of a culture that was built up over three-quarters of a century. Stalinism severely damaged that culture and we live, frankly, still in the shadow of the damage that was done. These sorts of issues are going to be absolutely indispensable in the rebuilding of a socialist culture, in the broadest sense.

DVR: I think the function of a critic, any critic, is partially that, of a preservator. That is to say, whatever emerges, it would be nice if the cultural heritage that we have managed to accumulate be handed on more or less intact. I think most modernists and even some of the post-modernists agree that the continuity in the arts is a very critical question. That's not just for a revolutionary party, but any honest critic. When you see something new, to be able to relate it to what's gone before. As well as to be able to see it within the context of the social forces at work.

If more artists were aware of the pressures that were on them, or influencing them, some of them would probably change what they were doing, and some of them would do what they are doing, but better. It's not enough that the dialectic recognizes the artist, even if the artist doesn't recognize the dialectic. It's true, but it's not enough.

DW: To get back to the chronology, how did you experience the 1980s?

DVR: Since the late 1970s I've been fighting a successful holding action. Two steps forward, two steps back. The thing you have to remember is that no one in their right mind ever got into this business because they thought they were going to get rich. My initial plan was to make a living. And, as far as I'm concerned, I've done it. "So far, so good," as the Irishman who fell off the Empire State Building, passing the thirtieth floor, was heard to say. What I measure my progress by isn't my standard of living. I've made a great deal of money when my output was really stagnant, and I have been really hard pressed when I'm going through a good period. Over all, I've grown a great deal, as a musician, as a singer. I'm so much more in command of my faculties at this stage of the game than I ever was before. That to me is an important thing.

DW: That was my feeling when I saw the performance in Ann Arbor. You reach a point where the secondary issues fall away and you speak very directly and very personally, and very honestly to people.

DVR: It's possible. That can be done. You don't have to create a phony persona. You need a persona, you cannot be exactly the same person on stage as you are off. But you have to construct your persona honestly. It's got to be made out of stuff that's really there. And sorting that business out takes a long, long time. It requires a certain amount of introspection. It requires a great deal of trial and error, and it requires, again, persistence.

What excites me is doing things musically that I would never have dreamt I could do even 10 years ago. Writing, working on new arrangements, this, that and the other thing. That's what keeps me going. Working on something that interests me, it's that puzzle aspect, making those damn things fit, putting it together so it's some kind of a coherent whole. That's a lot of fun. I'm very lucky, I happened to fall into a field where I can actually make a living doing what I like. There aren't too many people who do that. It's sheer luck. Absolutely. If I could have fallen by the wayside, I would have, any number of times. What if I had gotten rich in 1964? I don't know, probably, knowing myself I would have figured some way to get myself unrich quick. But what if I had? What if I were surrounded by a bunch of yes-men, who only told me what I wanted to hear, whether I asked them to do that or not, that's how it works. Or if the bottom had dropped out completely? What would have happened then?

DW: Is there any contemporary popular music that you like?

DVR: No, no field, there are individual performers. Singer/songwriters that I admire very much. But I wouldn't say that I like singer/songwriter music by and large. As somebody once said, 95 percent of everything is crap.

DW: Do you have any disappointments?

DVR: I really wish my ability to focus had been better. I don't think I've accomplished a tenth of what I could have. That irritates me. I get very annoyed with myself about that. When I see the kind of work I'm capable of doing under pressure. For example, I had to do two songs that I had never tried before on four days' notice, a couple of weeks ago. One of them was by Kurt Weill, the other I chose myself. It was Earl Robinson's I Dreamed I Saw Joe Hill Last Night.

Inside of three days I'd done it. I didn't have to chart the Weill song. It was Johnny's Song from Johnny Johnson. I thought they'd give me Lost in the Stars, September Song, the Bilbao Song, but, no, they gave me that dumb thing. It was hard, I was working from Weill's orchestral score. The Joe Hill song I'd never sung before. I had no idea what to do on the guitar. I did it as an encore the other night, in Oxford, New York. Thirty miles north of Binghamton. A full house of cows. Not a dry udder in the house.

I can do that kind of thing. And in theory I could have been doing that kind of thing for the last 30 years. I just don't have that single-mindedness, that focus. I could have done a lot more. But aside from that, no. I'm sorry I didn't do more and better of same.

Reprinted by with kind permission of David Walsh and the World Socialist Web Site (http://www.wsws.org). Interview conducted May 7th, 1998

A Dave Van Ronk Discography

1958 **The Orange Blossom Jug Five:**
Skiffle in Stereo
Lyrichord LLST 773

1959 **Dave Van Ronk Sings**
Ballads, Blues And A Spiritual
Folkways FS 3818
re-released on CD:
The Folkways Years, 1959 - 1961
Smithsonian Folkways CD 40041

1961 **Van Ronk Sings (Vol. 2)**
Folkways FA 2383

1963 **Dave Van Ronk, Folksinger**
Prestige 14012
re-released on CD as Fantasy CD 24710

1964 **Dave Van Ronk**
And The Red Onion Jazz Band:
In The Tradition
Prestige 14001

196? **Inside Dave Van Ronk**
Prestige/Folklore 14025
re-released on CD as Fantasy CD 24710

1964 **Just Dave Van Ronk**
Mercury 60808

1964 **Dave Van Ronk**
And The Ragtime Jug Stompers
Mercury SR 60864

1966 **No Dirty Names**
Verve/Forecast FTS 3009

1968 **Dave Van Ronk And The Hudson Dusters**
Verve/Forecast 3041

1971 **Van Ronk**
Polydor 24-4052

1973 **Songs For Ageing Children**
(Let The Feeling Talk To You)
Chess/Cadet CA 50044

1976 **Sunday Street**
Philo 1036
Rounder CD PHIL1036 (1986)

1980 **Somebody Else, Not Me**
Philo PH 1065 (rec. 1979)
Rounder CD PHIL1065 (1999)

1982 **Your Basic Dave Van Ronk**
Kicking Mule KM 177 (US)
Sonet 885 (UK)

1983 **St. James Infirmary**
Paris Album DKB 3359
re-released 1996 on CD: Statesboro Blues
EPM Musique BC157842

1985 **Going Back To Brooklyn**
Reckless RK 1916
re-released on CD: Gazell GPCD 2006 (1991)

1988 **Hesitation Blues**
Big Beat WIK 84
(Compilation from Prestige's "Folksinger",
"In The Tradition" and "Inside")

1990 **Frankie Armstrong & Dave Van Ronk:**
Let No One Deceive You
Songs of Bertolt Brecht
Flying Fish CD FF 70557

1990 **Peter & The Wolf**
Alacazam ALAC-CD 1004

1990 **Hummin' To Myself**
Dave Van Ronk Sings
An American Songbook
Gazell GPCD 2004

1991 **The Folkways Years, 1959 - 1961**
Smithsonian Folkways CD 40041

1992 **A Chrestomathy**
Gazell GPCD 2007/8
Compilation from early and recent
(1960 until 1991) records

1994 **To All My Friends In Far-Flung Places**
Gazell GPCD 2011/12

1995 **from ... another time & place**
Alcazar CD ALC 120

1997 **Dave Van Ronk**
Live at Sir George Williams University
Just A Memory CD 9132

Stefan Wirz (Hallerstr. 28, D-30161
Hannover, Germany http://www.wirz.de)
has compiled an extensive and complete
discography of Dave Van Ronk's solo
albums as well as other albums
where he is featured as a sideman.

Photo by Jo Ayres

9

EXPLANATION OF THE TAB SYSTEM

"…Learning from listening is unquestionably the best way, the only way that suits this kind of music. You are setting the notes down for a record of what happened, a record that can be studied, preserved and so on, a necessary and useful companion to the recordings of the actual sounds. I keep thinking of this as I transcribe; if you could do it, it would be good to have a legend across each page reading : 'Listen to the record if you want to learn the song.'"

Hally Wood (taken from the Publisher's Foreword to the *New Lost City Ramblers Songbook*.)

These words are most suitable for introducing the tablature system, for tablature is just a guide and should be used in conjunction with the recordings. Tablature is not like music notation, however the combination of tab and music in an arrangement forms a complete language. Used together with the original recordings they give a total picture of the music.

The tab system does not attempt to show rhythms or accents. These can be found on the music or heard in the recordings. Music notation tackles these articulations to a degree, but the overall sensations, the feel and the soul of music cannot be wholly captured on the written page. In the words of the great Sufi Hazrat Inayat Khan: "…The traditional ancient songs of India composed by great Masters have been handed down from father to son. The way music is taught is different from the Western way. It is not always written, but is taught by imitation. The teacher sings and the pupil imitates and the intricacies and subtleties are learned by imitation."

This is the theme I've tried to interpolate into the tablature. Tablature is the roadmap and you are the driver. Now to the tab:

Each space indicates a string. The top space represents the first string, second space the second string, etc. A zero means an open string, a number in the space indicates the fretted position, for instance a 1 in a space indicates the first fret of that string.

In the diagram below the zero is on the second string and indicates the open second string is played. The 1 is placed on the third string and signifies the first fret of the third string. Likewise, the 4 is in the fourth space and indicates the fourth fret of the fourth string.

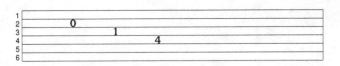

Generally for fingerpicking styles you will be playing the thumb, index and middle fingers of your picking hand. To indicate the picking finger in tab the stems go up and line up down from the numbers.

A. A stem down means that your thumb strikes the note.
B. If a stem is up, your index or middle finger strikes the note. The choice of finger is left up to you, as your fingers will dictate what is most comfortable, especially when playing a song up to tempo!

C. The diagram below shows an open sixth string played with the thumb followed by the second fret of the third string played with the index or middle finger:

In most cases the thumb will play an alternating bass pattern, usually on the bass strings. The index and middle fingers play melodic notes on the first, second and third strings. Please remember, this is not a rule; there are many exceptions.

In fingerpicking there are two "picking" styles: Regular picking and "pinching" two notes together. A pinch is shown in the tab by a line connecting two notes. A variation of this can also be two treble notes pinched with a bass note. Follow the examples below from left to right:

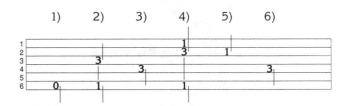

1) The open sixth string is played with the thumb.
2) The first fret of the sixth string is pinched together with the third fret on the third string. The sixth string is played with the thumb, the third string with the index finger.
3) The thumb strikes the third fret of the fourth string.
4) The first fret/sixth string is played with the thumb; it's pinched with two notes in the treble. The index and middle fingers strike the first fret/first string and the third fret/second string.
5) The next note is the index finger hitting the first fret/second string.
6) Lastly, the bass note is played with the thumb on the third fret/fourth string.

There are certain places in blues and contemporary guitar that call for the use of either strumming techniques or accented bass notes. The tab illustrates these as follows:

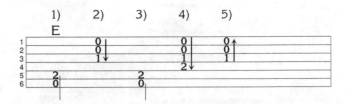

1) The thumb hits the open sixth string and the second fret on the fifth string should also sound. For example, play an E chord. Now strike the open string and vary the force of your attack. Try hitting it hard enough so that the fifth string vibrates as well. This technique is very important for developing a full sound and the right alternating bass sound.

2) Next the arrow notation indicates a brush and the arrowhead indicates the direction of the brush.

   A. If the arrowhead is pointed down, the hand brushes up towards the sixth string.
   B. If pointed up, the hand brushes down towards the first string.
   C. The number of strings to be played by the brush is shown by the length of the arrows. For example, this arrow shows a brush up toward the sixth string, but indicates to strike only the first, second and third strings.
   D. The brush can be done with your whole hand, index finger or middle and ring finger. Let comfort plus a full and "right" sound guide your choice.

3) The third set of notes again shows the sixth string/open bass note played with the thumb and being struck hard enough to make the fifth string/second fretted position sound.

4) Once more an arrow pointed downward indicates a brush up. This example forms an E chord and the brush up includes the first, second, third and fourth strings.

5) The last set of notes has an arrow pointed upward, indicating a brush downward striking the first, second, and third strings.

Here are several special effects that are also symbolized in tablature:

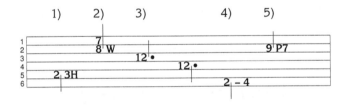

1) HAMMER-ON: Designated by an "H" which is placed after the stem on the fret to be hammered. In the example above, fret the second fret/fifth string and pick it with your thumb. Then "hammer-on" (hit hard) the third fret/fifth string, i.e. fret the third fret/fifth string. This is an all-in-one, continuous motion which will produce two notes rapidly with one picking finger strike.

2) WHAM: Designated by a "W." In the example the eighth fret/second string is "whammed" and played with the seventh fret/first string. Both notes are played together with your index and middle fingers respectively. The whammed note is "stretched." We do this by literally bending the note up. We can "wham" the note up a half tone, full tone, etc.

3) HARMONICS: Symbolized by a dot (•). To play a harmonic: gently lay your finger directly above the indicated fret (don't press down!) The two notes in the example are both harmonics. The first on the twelfth fret/third string is played with the index/middle finger, while the second note—twelfth fret/fourth string—is played with the thumb.

4) SLIDE: Shown with a dash (–). Play the second fret/sixth string and then slide up to the fourth fret of the sixth string. This is a continuous movement: the string is struck once with your thumb.

5) PULL-OFF: "P" designates a "pull-off." Fret both the seventh and ninth frets on the second string. Play the ninth fret with your index/middle finger and then quickly remove it in the same stroke, leaving the seventh fret/second string. Pull-offs are generally in a downward direction.

6) In certain cases other specific symbols are added to the tab, for instance:
   A. For ARTIFICIAL HARMONICS an "X" is placed after the fretted position.
   B. For SNAPPING a note an indication may be given with a symbol or the written word.

Many times these special techniques are combined, for instance putting a pull-off and a hammer-on together. Coordination of your fretting and picking hands will be complex initially, but the end results are exciting and fun to play.

PICKING HAND POSITION FOR FINGERPICKING STYLES: The Classical and Flamenco schools have strict right-hand rules, however for this style of acoustic fingerpicking there are NO RULES, only suggestions. Your right hand position should be dictated by comfort, however in observation of many well-known fingerpickers I found one hand position similarity—they all tend to rest their little finger and/or ring finger on the face of the guitar. This seems to help their balance for accenting notes and control of the guitar. Experiment with this position: it may feel uncomfortable at first. I ask my students to perfect this position and then compare the sound to when their finger(s) were not placed on the face of the guitar. They usually find the sound is greatly improved when some contact is kept with the guitar face.

MUSIC NOTATION: We have somewhat adapted the music notation in that this also shows whether the note is picked with your thumb or index/middle fingers. The stems of the music notes correspond to the direction of the tab stems. I hope this will make the music notation clearer to fingerpicking guitarists.

I hope you will feel at home and comfortable with the tablature and musical notations. Remember, these are only road maps indicating where and how you should place your fingers. The playing and musical interpretation is up to you.

GREEN, GREEN, ROCKY ROAD

Drop D Tuning, DADGBE

L. Chandler / R. Kaufman

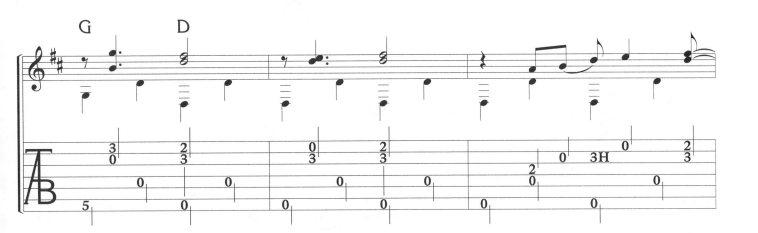

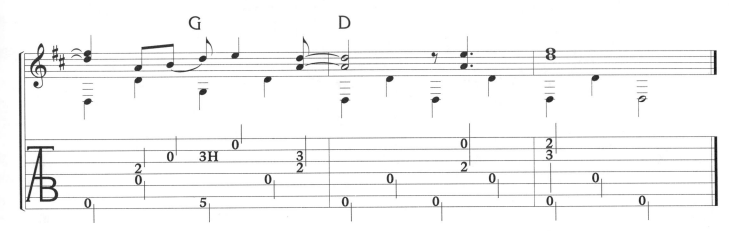

Photo by Jo Ayres

13

KANSAS CITY BLUES

Drop D Tuning, DADGBE

Traditional

14

SATURDAY NIGHT SHUFFLE

Standard Tuning

Merle Travis

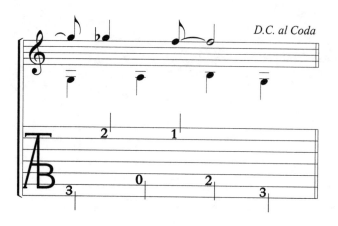

D.C. al Coda

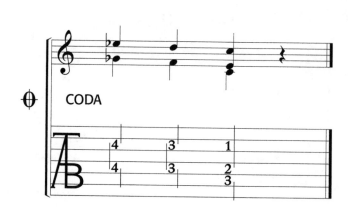

CODA

STACKERLEE

Standard Tuning

Traditional — Arranged by Dave Van Ronk

GUITAR BREAK

Photo by Jo Ayres

Dave Van Ronk & Stefan Grossman

18

BALLAD OF THE IRT

Standard Tuning

Traditional – Lyrics by Lawrence Block

WILSON RAG

Elizabeth Cotten

Standard Tuning

Photo by Jo Ayres

22

THAT WILL NEVER HAPPEN NO MORE

Standard Tuning

Traditional

23

24

SPIKE DRIVER'S MOAN

Standard Tuning

J. Hurt

(G)

25

Sportin' Life Blues

Drop D Tuning, DADGBE

B. McGhee

26

St. James Infirmary

Standard Tuning

Traditional

29

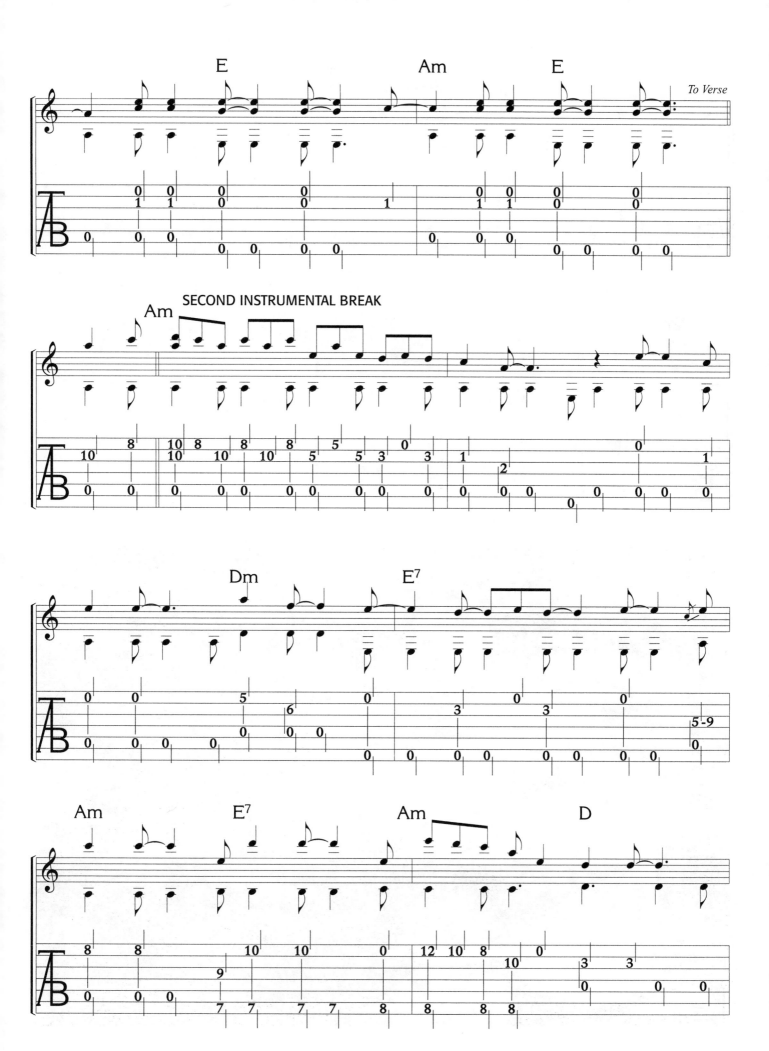

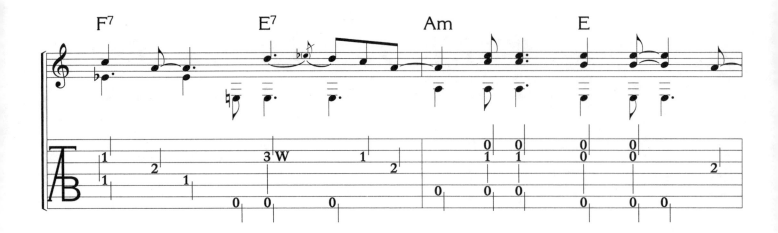

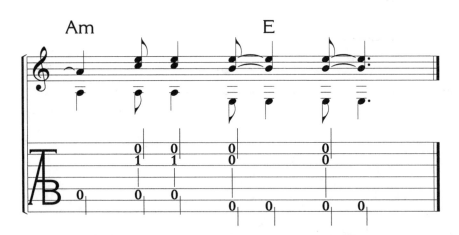

Photo by Jo Ayres